BASIC
FLOWER
DESIGN

MARTA DE PAZ

Floral Design Instructor

Andrew Benzie Books
Walnut Creek, California

Published by Andrew Benzie Books
www.andrewbenziebooks.com

Printed in the United States of America

ISBN 978-1-941713-53-2

martas_flowers@yahoo.com

Cover & book design by Andrew Benzie

Dedicated to Natalia Trabanino and Ann Nakatani

with deep love and appreciation

Table of Contents

Flower Arrangements

Flower Arranging

General Guidelines

The pre-requisite for a flower designer is simply a love for flowers.

- Cut stems at an angle—keep flowers in floral preservative mixed with water.
- Hard woody stems—cut at an angle then cut one inch slit up each stem or you may hammer the end of the stem.
- Milky stems—cut at an angle, cover flower with tissue or plastic. Hold ends in a match or gas flame for a few seconds.

NOTE:
- If hydrangeas wilt, renew by putting flower heads in water.
- Reviving flowers after a few days: Boil water, protect flower heads, place bottom stems (1 inch) into water for 20 seconds, then place flowers in tepid floral food water nearly up to the flower.
- For most arrangements everything should radiate from a central point without crossing the stems.
- Select flowers in various stages, buds to fully open blooms.
- Do not overcrowd—"leave room for the butterfly."
- Create a focal point. If desired using the most dominant flowers, strongest color and larger leaves.
- All leaves should be removed below the water line.
- The warmer the water, the faster the flower will bloom. The best way is to order your flowers prior to use and allow them to open naturally. Each flower opens differently, depending on the time of the year and the conditions they have been kept in prior to your use.

Arrangement Preparation

- Preservative: food for flowers (pH balance)
- Clean vase—no soap residue
- Use oasis, chicken wire, frog, floral tape
- Remove leaves below the water line
- Slant cut the bottom of the stems
- Always store and transport flowers in water when possible
- Re-cut each time flower is out of water
- The warmer the water, the faster the flowers bloom. Best to plan on the time needed to allow the flowers to bloom naturally.
- Put green in first to set the line
- Use paper towel as a non-skid mat at the bottom of oasis (for highly glazed surface)

Using Bud Vase

- Use bud vase—fill with treated water
- Add flowers 1 > 2 > 3 (vary height)
- Add foliage near rim of vase
- Add line of foliage or flowers behind massed flowers (keeps flowers securely in place)
- Filler flowers & foliage may be added to complete and give accent to design
- Add bow in front of rim to serve as accent—also may add Bear Grass

Circular Design

The round arrangement shape appears the same on all sides and from all viewing angles. This design is also called round mound, nosegay, and tussie-mussie. Because there is no front or back, this design offers more versatility in placement. A fine foliage adds a certain contrast to the dominant round flower forms.

Steps in Construction

- Soak oasis in water.
- Cut foam to fit round container. Cut off corners and round the oasis on top. Secure foam with waterproof tape.
- If desired, pre-green. The greens at the edges of the container should be placed at a downward angle to cover the rim of the container. If you arrange the green leaves first, follow the next 3-8 guidelines and then go back and place the flowers.
- Place a flower or bud in the center to establish height.
- Insert flowers near the rim of the container that extend out horizontally or slightly downward to establish width on the 4 sides (north, south, east, west).
- Insert the next row up higher and in between the rim flowers and again use the (4) flowers using the north, south, east & west guideline.
- Continue moving up to the top. Moving higher and in between each lower flower group.
- All flowers should be the same length and appear to be radiating from the center.
- Add filler.

NOTE:
- Move your arrangement away from you.
- Step back and look at it from a distance. Does it look right to you?
- Turn and look at it again and again. Adjust as necessary.
- This is a good thing to do with all of your arrangements.

Vase Arrangements

Vase arrangements are designed with mass, form, and line flowers as well as mass, form and line greenery and/or accessories/filler. There are Vase creations that range from very large designs to just a bud vase.

Definitions

Mass adds mass (bulk and weight) quickly. If used alone, vary color, size, spacing and depth.

Form Interesting, distinctive, and captivating shapers. Often used at or near rim or container (use as a direction for eye to follow).

Line linear shape—generally tall and long—several blossoms can create height, width and depth and are placed first when used.

Grid

Directions

1. Using medium to large vases, remove all greenery below the water line.

2. Add all greenery first—all around—crisscrossing stems. Add some filler in the same fashion.

3. Add flowers, more foliage and filler—forming a grid.

4. Use flowers, fillers, and foliage with strong stems.

Wreath History

In Greek or Roman times, a wreath on the head symbolized honor, and a wreath of laurel was presented in honor of special achievement.

Andria Della Robbia was an Italian artist. The "Della Robbia" style is a wreath of real fruit and leaves. This artist lived from 1435 to 1525 and two of his wreaths hang in New York City's Metropolitan Museum of Art.

The Goddess of Spring is enwreathed with flowers. Botticellie's "Primavera" shows this very thing (Renaissance Faire).

Colonial-American wreaths included the use of fresh fruits, those that grew locally or for wealthier people, those that were imported. Placement of the materials was highly organized and symmetrical. Fresh fruits and greens enhance the rich textures of dried cones and pods. In keeping with the true colonial style, use mostly local materials.

The Victorian style of decorating was abundant, often overflowing with a romantic feel. Flowered arched garlands graced the areas between dining room and parlor.

Note: when making a Victorian style wreath, use some faded flowers (roses stored several years in plastic bags lose most of their color but not their structure). Cockscomb and straw flowers in pale shades give the impression of age.

Contemporary flair—Eight feet of copper refrigerator tubing costs less than good ribbon and can serve the same purpose on a wreath.

TIP: Strive for creativity.

Mini Carnation Arrangement

- 12 stems elegant miniature carnations
- 12 stems leatherleaf
- number 18 and 28 green wire for leatherleaf
- number 16 and 26 green wire for carnation stem
- 1 block floral foam
- vinyl mending tape
- clear tape to stabilize form
- goblet container–4" diameter x 6" height

Standard Carnation and Eucalyptus Triangular Arrangement

- 12 standard carnations
- 10 to 12 stems of eucalyptus
- number 16 wire and 26 wire for eucalyptus
- number 18 wire and 28 wire for carnations
- extender if carnation is short
- 1 cube of floral foam
- vinyl tape
- clear tape
- 5" diameter and 10" tall circle cylindrical glass vase

Half-Circle Basket Arrangement

- green button pompons
- white daisy pompons
- hot pink mini carnations
- purple carnations
- 6 stem leatherleaf
- number 20 wire and number 26 wire for pom pon mums
- number 18 and number 28 wire for leatherleaf and carnations
- number 26 wire to tie floral foam to basket
- basket—6" diameter x 4" deep with liner

Standard Rose Arrangement

- 12 stems standard roses
- 12 stems of leatherleaf
- 6 stems of myrtus communis (mini myrtle)
- number 16 wire and number 26 wire for roses
- number 18 wire and number 28 wire for leatherleaf
- vinyl tape
- no floral foam is used in this arrangement
- randall rose vase

Sweetheart Short-Stem Baby Roses Half-Circle Arrangement

- 12 stems of sweetheart roses
- 4 stems of huckleberry
- 4 stems of leatherleaf
- 4 stems of gypsophilia (baby's breath)
- number 18 and number 28 wire for leatherleaf and carnations
- vinyl tape
- number 20 wire and number 22 or 24 wire for gypsophilia (baby's breath)
- 1 block floral foam
- 1 glass goblet—3.5 to 4" in diameter and 6" tall

Two Candle Mixed Flower Table Centerpiece

- 4 standard carnations
- 4 stems daisy mum
- 6 stems pom pon mum
- 4 cushion chrysanthemum
- 6 stems leatherleaf
- 2 stems huckleberry
- 1 15" candle
- center piece container 8" x 3.5" x 2.5" deep
- 1 same size floral foam
- vinyl tape for candle
- clear tape for container
- suitable wire as needed

Basket Arrangement with Fruit

- 2 stems gladiolas
- 3 pink roses
- 3 stems of orange spray roses
- 2 stems lemon leaf
- 3 strings ivy
- 1 basket 12" wide x 8" depth
- 1 container liner
- 1 block floral foam
- 3 bunches of grapes, 3 pears, 3 apples, 3 oranges, 3 bananas, 1 pineapple & assorted nuts
- number 16, 18, 20, 22, 24, 26, and 28 wires for stems
- green and brown tapes, vinyl tape and clear tape

Daisy Arrangement

- 6 yellow roses
- 4 stems white daisy pom mums
- 6 stems green button pom mums
- 6 stems yellow alstroemeria
- 4 stems leatherleaf
- 1 basket 7" diameter x 4" high with 12" tall handle
- 1 basket liner 7" diameter and 4" high
- 1 floral foam or 10" cylinder vase
- number 18, 20 or 22, and 28 wires
- 2 yards of number 3 ribbon

Baby Gift Triangular Arrangement

Baby First Block—Blue
• yellow daisies
• white spray roses
• blue delphinium
• blue ribbon
• glass baby block vase

Baby First Block—Pink
• pink gerbera daisies
• white spray roses
• pink spray roses
• monte casino
• glass baby block vase

Triangle Arrangement
• pom pon daisies
• pink alstroemeria
• lavender
• pink carnations
• glass baby block vase

Other Supplies
• 1 block floral foam
• number 18, 20, 24, 28 wires
• vinyl tape
• clear tape
• 5" square container

Half-Circle Mixed Flower Arrangement

- 5 standard carnations
- 6 stems yellow button pom pon
- 4 stems orange mini carnation
- 4 stems fushia mini carnation
- 4 stems statice
- 8 stems of leatherleaf
- number 18, 20, 22, 24, 28 wires
- 1 block of floral foam
- 10" diameter x 5" tall round flower vase or basket
- vinyl and clear tapes

Rose and Carnation Spectacular Arrangement

- 6 carnations
- 6 medium stem roses
- 6 galax leaf
- 6 eucalyptus stems
- 5" diameter x 5" tall circle flower vase
- 1 cube floral foam
- vinyl tape
- number 16, 18, 28 wires

A Get Well Arrangement

- 5 standard carnations
- 5 stems mini carnations
- 3 roses
- 3 liatris or stocks
- 6 galax leaf
- 1 basket 13" long x 8" wide x 5" deep
- liner
- 2 cubes floral foam
- number 16, 18, 26, 28 wires

High-Style with Oriental Flair

- 2 lionmane papyrus or bamboo sticks
- 3 gerberas
- 3 stems lily buds
- 3 stems euphorbia or queen ann's lace
- 2 stems of statice
- 2 tea leaf
- 5 galax leaf
- 10" or 12" diameter x 4" deep round moribana vase

The Height of Sophistication with Oriental Flair

- high-style temple container or any look-alike oriental vase
- 2 stems fuji mum
- 2 stems lily
- 1 stem curly willow
- 2 lycopodium
- 2 gladiola foliage
- 2 big mushrooms
- 1 cube floral foam
- 1 small bag of moss
- number 16, 18, 26, 28 wires
- brown tape
- vinyl tape

Dish Garden

- philodendron plant
- dracaena plant
- spathiphyllum plant
- palm plant
- 2 stems alstroemevia
- dish for planting container or
  a rectangular basket 12" or 14"
- planting charcoal
- planting mix soil
- 2 extenders

A Traditional Spray

- pink carnations
- white chrysanthemums
- seasonal roses
- decorative ribbon
- leatherleaf and palm leaf

Other Materials and Supplys
- 1 plastic container 16" wide x 4" high and 4" depth or one small oasis floracage
- 2 cubes floral foam
- vinyl and clear tapes
- number 15, 18, 26, 28 wires

Wreath with Fresh or Silk

- wreath—10" to 12" diameter
- pink roses
- oriental lilies
- gladiolus
- hydrangea
- carnations
- lush green
- number 20, 22, 24, 26, 28 wire and number 16 and 18 wire for stems
- glue guns and sticks
- heavy duty wire cutter is necessary for silk wreath

Symmetrical Triangle Design

Pink Carnation Triangle Arrangement
- A dozen standard carnations
- 6 stems of eucalyptus
- lypocodium

Mixed Flower Triangle Arrangement
- 5 roses
- 6 oriental lilies
- 6 stems daisy mums
- leatherleaf
- gladiola leaves

Other Materials and Supplys
- 1 round container 10" to 12" diameter and 4" depth
- floral foam
- vinyl tape
- number 16, 18, 20, 26, 28 wire

High-Style with Gladiolus and Carnations Double-Image

- 1 round container 10" to 12" diameter x 4" deep
- 6 stems gladioli
- 6 miniature carnations
- 4 stems hackberry leaf
- 6 standard carnations
- 2 cubes floral foam

Agapanthus
Year-Round

Alstroemeria
Year-Round

Amaranthus
August-December

Amaryllis
October-April

Anemone
November-May

Anthurium
Year-Round

Bells of Ireland
Year-Round

Bird of Paradise
Year-Round

Bouvardia
Year-Round

Bupleurem
Year-Round

Button Pompon
Year-Round

Calla Lily
Year-Round

Carnation – Mini
Year-Round

Carnation – Standard
Year-Round

Celosia
July-September

Chinaberry
September-November

Matsumoto Aster
Year-Round

Monte Casino
Year-Round

Orchid – Cymbidium
Year-Round

Orchid – Dendrobium
Year-Round

Orchid – Mokara
Year-Round

Orchid – Oncidium
Year-Round

Orchid – Phalaenopsis
Year-Round

Peony
April-June

Phlox
Year-Round

Poppy
February-May

Protea – Mink
Year-Round

Protea – Pincushion
March-September

Pussy Willow
January-April

Queen Anne's Lace
Year-Round

Ranunculus
February-May

Red Rover Chrysanthemum
August-November

Rose
Year-Round

Snapdragon
Year-Round

Solidago
Year-Round

Spray Rose
Year-Round

Star of Bethlehem
October-May

Statice
Year-Round

Stephanotis
January-November

Stock
Year-Round

Sunflower
Year-Round

Sweet Pea
March-July

Tulip
Year-Round

Tulip – Parrot
February-May

Veronica
Year-Round

Viburnum
January-April

Waxflower
Year-Round

Yellow Yarrow
July-November

Made in United States
North Haven, CT
07 October 2023